YES, #WatchMe I CAN

A Space For Girls To Build Brave And Powerful Confidence, Self Esteem And Self-Love

FROM AMAZON-BEST SELLING AUTHOR

Courtney St Croix

Yes, I Can
#WatchMe

Cover and all interior designs by Courtney St Croix
Photography by Hilary Spencer

ISBN: 978-1-9993857-2-9
Published by: THINK Yourself® PUBLISHING

For more information, visit www.MomfidentAF.com,
find @MomfidentAF on Instagram, or email hello@MomfidentAF.com

For Presley, Rachel, and Brynley.

You are capable, you are worthy, you are strong, and you are loved.
You can do anything, and I can't wait to watch.

How to use this journal:
A note to incredible parents and guardians

Hello, incredible parent and equally-as-incredible sweet girl. Before you dive into this journal, it's important to know a few things about the process and the questions. The next few pages will give you some insight into to how to best use this journal: how to set your daughter up for success, some of the reasons why this journal was designed, and why these questions and activities were selected.

The journal is intended for all girls, as long as they are able to read (the questions), comprehend (what the questions ask them to do), and write (put their thoughts together on paper). This may require guidance, or perhaps they will practice on their own. I do encourage you to get involved and be part of the process, but I also trust that you will be able to determine if your daughter is able to comprehend the content, is better suited to journaling privately, or if she welcomes parental engagement and insight, regardless of her age.

You may need to define some of the common terms used throughout the workbook, so I've done that for you in the space below. For example, before starting, it's worth having a discussion about what gratitude means, so they can understand what types of answers they can fill in for that question and get better at noticing things they're grateful for.

As our sweet girls get into junior and intermediate school ages, research shows that their self-esteem and confidence declines substantially. This is not only in comparison to boys of the same age, but the percentage gap is equally as important. According to a self-esteem study published in a 1996 edition of the *New York Times*, "Girls emerge from adolescence with a poor self-image, relatively low expectations from life and much less confidence in themselves and their abilities than boys". **1**

In the transition between elementary age to high school age, most girls feel less confident and happy with themselves. When asked if they felt happy with themselves, 60 percent of girls in elementary school responded "always." That number drops to 29 percent with the transition to high school. **1**

I would argue that the lack of confidence and the decrease in self-esteem in our girls is even worse now, considering that 1996 did not come with the same technology and media influences that prevail now. According to a study conducted for the benefit of the Dove Self-Esteem Project, social media has the potential to negatively affect a girl's self-esteem, for a number of different reasons. Most notably, the potential for regular comparison of themselves to others, and the fact that social media offers a false sense of reality. **2**.

So, I think you'd agree that it's time we start proactively focusing on this concerning trend. Pre-teen is the perfect age to start introducing tried-and-true strategies, like positive affirmations, gratitude, and the practice of stating things they love about themselves out loud (or at least on paper!) I encourage you to get involved in this practice, and discuss gratitude, loving yourself, accepting your body, non-comparison, imperfection, and embracing uniqueness with your daughter as consistently as you can.

Okay, so now what?

In order for your sweet girl to start practicing with this workbook, you'll need to explain and discuss some of the key terms and concepts. This will vary depending on your daughter's age, so you may need to have a discussion about this journal and why it can and will benefit her.

Full disclosure, fellow guardian:

This part may look "boring" and "research-y", but I highly encourage you to fully absorb this section before you introduce this powerful journaling practice to your daughter. This is the "why" behind the act of writing answers to questions on a daily basis. And, (this is important) as a disclaimer, the information provided in this workbook is not intended to treat, cure, or diagnose any psychological or physiological condition, and is not a replacement for medical care, treatment, or guidance from a medical professional. I am *not* a doctor. I'm just a woman committed to bettering herself and the world around her by creating spaces for females to focus on their greatness.

Enter: creating a mom-focused Self-Love Journal, and the follow up: THIS JOURNAL. This journal is intended as a proactive and complementary addition to a well-rounded well-being practice, with the sole purpose of helping a young girl understand her worth and her value, and to focus on her strengths and her positive qualities for the betterment of her self-image.

Alright, now here's the "technical" reason why each topic/section is included in the journal pages:

Something I love about myself TODAY: This question is designed to have your sweet girl start thinking about her incredible qualities. Not just an external trait, like "I love my eyes". That may be how it starts, but the object here is for her to start recognizing things she loves about her personality, her character, her skills, her talents, her abilities… the qualities that remain unchanged whether her external appearance does or does not. These are the things that contribute to high self-esteem, strong self-worth, and a self-love that's deeper than just being happy with your hair or your smile.

Gratitude: Regularly practicing gratitude, stating things you're grateful for, and consistently writing them down, has been scientifically shown to improve psychological health and well-being. Bringing awareness to the good things in your life can proactively shift the mindset to one more conducive to positivity, openness, happiness and fulfillment.

A study published in the *Journal of Applied Sport Psychology* found that "gratitude increased athletes' self-esteem" and "reduces social comparisons. Rather than becoming resentful toward people who have more money or better jobs—a major factor in reduced self-esteem—grateful people are able to appreciate other people's accomplishments." **3.**

Kindness: The benefits of practicing kindness to ourselves and to others are insurmountable and go a long way to assist with the health and well-being of an individual, especially a young girl. According to an article on "The Science of Kindness" from the Random Acts of Kindness Foundation, there are proven benefits to being kind which include the fact that kindness is teachable and contagious, requires no skill or ability, and is always available. The article specifically lists that kindness "increases the love hormone, increases energy and happiness, increases lifespan, pleasure, and the production of the body's "feel good" hormone, serotonin." Practicing kindness regularly can also "decrease pain, stress, anxiety and blood pressure" and has even been linked to decreased rates of depression. **4.**

Physical Strength: Multiple influences in our media-overloaded world often tell a girl the most important thing about her is what she looks like, how "skinny" she is, what size she wears, and how closely she resembles the images she sees in the media. This is distorting our girls' body image and sends confusing messages about their self-worth. The point of this section is to link physical activity with making our bodies stronger, *not* so that we can force our bodies to look a certain way on the outside. It is meant only to open the door to the fact that physical movement helps our bodies to become strong and healthy, and that should be the ultimate goal for body movement, fitness, and sports, *not* just what may happen to her body on the outside if she is active.

Affirmations: The things we think about ourselves become the things we believe about ourselves. Negative self-talk plagues women of all ages, so building a positive self-talk practice at a young age has the potential to positively impact a girl and her self-esteem beyond measure. Affirmations are simply positive statements that are written or spoken in the present tense, as if they are already true.

For example, an affirmation like "I *am* beautiful" is far more powerful than declaring "I *will be* beautiful" which is then dependent on external or various future factors in order to be true. When statements like this are repeated consistently, they have the power to re-wire the brain and the thought patterns inside the brain. Over time, even if she doesn't think she *is* beautiful right now, she will likely start to believe it with enough practice. The mind will believe what we tell it, so proactively stating positive things about ourselves sets us up for long-term and optimistic mindset success.

Sharing Feelings: Children need to know that having different emotions and feelings are okay, and that having an open space to share their good, bad, or ugly feelings is important. They may feel less inclined to share *verbally* with someone, (even if there is a trusted source around them, like you, dear parent) but there is a chance they would feel safer if they can get their feelings down on paper, then at least they're out and not stuck swirling around inside. Having a safe and designated outlet to allow and respectfully process her feelings, whether she realizes she is doing that or not, is an important component to overall mental health.

Weekly Reflection: Being able to easily acknowledge that there will always be peaks and valleys in life allows for us to better cope with difficult moments and stages. The weekly reflection is designed to help her understand that she is powerful enough to get through whatever challenge she faces, and that she can identify that there are both good and not-so-good experiences, but that she can get through them always.

Part of the weekly reflection is a mindfulness activity that is meant to encourage girls to learn to effectively cope with stress, anxiety, and the challenges of life. The Centre for Mindfulness Studies defines mindfulness as a practice to "train ourselves to pay close attention to what is going on in the present moment; just as it is. Much of our suffering is a result of regrets about the past, worries about the future or judgments about the present. When we are mindful we become aware of and explore these habitual thought patterns and ways of reacting. This attitude of curiosity allows us to create new and healthier ways of responding to life's challenges." **5.**

Okay, let her go!

Now that you've gotten through the "why", it may be time to have a discussion about the "how" with your sweet girl. Start by asking her the questions and gauge whether she understands or needs clarification. Once she understands what is required, discuss with her how often she'd like to try using the journal, and allow her the freedom to choose the way that feels most comfortable for her. There is no right or wrong way to use this journal. Gentle encouragement may help or hinder the process, so be sure to allow her the space to experiment with it and see if it's right for her. She is unique, after all.

Hello, sweet girl.

You are the most unique human being in this world. Did you know that? There is nobody (*like, nobody!*) who is exactly like you. You were created on purpose, and your uniqueness and individuality is *exactly* what makes you special. You may have things in common with your BFFs, or maybe you don't. You may have similar physical traits as your bestie, or maybe not. I want you to know that *no matter what you look like* on the outside, you are loved, you are valuable, your opinion matters, and you are more powerful than you'll ever know. There is nothing valuable in looking exactly the same as everybody else. You were born to stand out.

You are growing up in a world that constantly shoves unrealistic expectations at you. A world where social media connects you with cool people from around the world, but also has the ability to make you think you need to look like someone on Instagram who has been photoshopped and edited.

Real people have flaws. You have flaws. I have flaws. We all have them, and it's what makes this world amazing. Embrace your flaws. Embrace your imperfections. Embrace your strong body. There is no body that is more perfect than another. There is no girl who is more capable or talented than another. We are all unique in our own ways, and we are all capable of accomplishing our goals. This workbook is designed to help you tap into your uniqueness and create magic.

Magic? Yes. Magic. Because when you feel confident with yourself, when you're comfortable with who you are, when you have the courage to respectfully say what you think without fear and are brave enough to put your hand up…that's when the magic happens. That's when you learn how to be the best, strongest, and most impactful girl in the world, who grows up to be a powerful young woman. And that's when you learn how to empower other girls just like you, to be who *they* are, and proud of it.

We are all strong.
We are all unique.
We all have something to say.
We are all capable of being kind - to ourselves, and to our fellow girls.

So let's take a stand. Let's create a powerful, positive mindset, so that we can help shape the confidence and self-esteem of our friends and sisters, too. Let's show the world that loving ourselves for our uniqueness, flaws, strengths, and imperfections, is the most important thing we'll ever learn to do.

I see you, sweet girl. Let's go.

YES, #WatchMe I CAN

DATE: June 6th 2019

Something I love about myself TODAY:

My Humor!

Something I am grateful for TODAY: (Focus on people, relationships, places, experiences - not "things.")

Owen, Kate, Carter

I will practice kindness to someone else TODAY by (doing)/saying/acting:

Hugging my bestie!

To make my body strong TODAY, I will:

Participate In gym. Praise myself "I am brave"

Re-write the following affirmations in the space under each phrase:

I AM KIND AND CAPABLE
I AM KIND AND CAPABLE!

MY BODY IS STRONG
MY BODY IS STRONG!

I AM BRAVE
I AM BRAVE!

I LOVE WHO I AM
I Love who I am!

I AM A BEAUTIFUL PERSON
I am a beautiful person!

I AM LOVED BY MANY
I am loved by many!

How was my day today? (*Great? Good? Hard? Why?*) If I felt a difficult feeling today, I will write it down here. Who can I ask for help with this feeling?

My day was great! I didn't have any difficult feelings. Just a really good, amazing, great day!

YES, I CAN. AND I WILL. WATCH ME.

YES,
#WatchMe
I CAN

DATE: _____

Something I love about myself TODAY:

[ ]

Something I am grateful for TODAY: (Focus on people, relationships, places, experiences - not "things.")

[ ]

I will practice kindness to someone else TODAY by doing/saying/acting:

[ ]

To make my body strong TODAY, I will:

[ ]

Re-write the following affirmations in the space <u>under</u> each phrase:

I AM KIND AND CAPABLE   MY BODY IS STRONG

I AM BRAVE   I LOVE WHO I AM

I AM A BEAUTIFUL PERSON   I AM LOVED BY MANY

How was my day today? (*Great? Good? Hard? Why?*) If I felt a difficult feeling today, I will write it down here. Who can I ask for help with this feeling?

[ ]

YES, I CAN. AND I WILL. WATCH ME.

YES, I CAN
#WatchMe

DATE: _____

Something I love about myself TODAY:

```
[                                                    ]
```

Something I am grateful for TODAY: (Focus on people, relationships, places, experiences - not "things.")

```
[                                                    ]
```

I will practice kindness to someone else TODAY by doing/saying/acting:

```
[                                                    ]
```

To make my body strong TODAY, I will:

```
[                                                    ]
```

Re-write the following affirmations in the space <u>under</u> each phrase:

I AM KIND AND CAPABLE   MY BODY IS STRONG

I AM BRAVE   I LOVE WHO I AM

I AM A BEAUTIFUL PERSON   I AM LOVED BY MANY

How was my day today? (*Great? Good? Hard? Why?*) If I felt a difficult feeling today, I will write it down here. Who can I ask for help with this feeling?

```
[                                                    ]
```

YES, I CAN. AND I WILL. WATCH ME.

YES, I CAN
#WatchMe

DATE: _____

Something I love about myself TODAY:

Something I am grateful for TODAY: (Focus on people, relationships, places, experiences - not "things.")

I will practice kindness to someone else TODAY by doing/saying/acting:

To make my body strong TODAY, I will:

Re-write the following affirmations in the space <u>under</u> each phrase:

I AM KIND AND CAPABLE   MY BODY IS STRONG

I AM BRAVE   I LOVE WHO I AM

I AM A BEAUTIFUL PERSON   I AM LOVED BY MANY

How was my day today? (*Great? Good? Hard? Why?*) If I felt a difficult feeling today, I will write it down here. Who can I ask for help with this feeling?

YES, I CAN. AND I WILL. WATCH ME.

YES,
#WatchMe
I CAN

DATE: _____

Something I love about myself TODAY:

Something I am grateful for TODAY: (Focus on people, relationships, places, experiences - not "things.")

I will practice kindness to someone else TODAY by doing/saying/acting:

To make my body strong TODAY, I will:

Re-write the following affirmations in the space <u>under</u> each phrase:

I AM KIND AND CAPABLE   MY BODY IS STRONG

I AM BRAVE   I LOVE WHO I AM

I AM A BEAUTIFUL PERSON   I AM LOVED BY MANY

How was my day today? (*Great? Good? Hard? Why?*) If I felt a difficult feeling today, I will write it down here. Who can I ask for help with this feeling?

YES, I CAN. AND I WILL. WATCH ME.

YES, I CAN
#WatchMe

DATE: _____

Something I love about myself TODAY:

Something I am grateful for TODAY: (Focus on people, relationships, places, experiences - not "things.")

I will practice kindness to someone else TODAY by doing/saying/acting:

To make my body strong TODAY, I will:

Re-write the following affirmations in the space <u>under</u> each phrase:

I AM KIND AND CAPABLE   MY BODY IS STRONG

I AM BRAVE   I LOVE WHO I AM

I AM A BEAUTIFUL PERSON   I AM LOVED BY MANY

How was my day today? (*Great? Good? Hard? Why?*) If I felt a difficult feeling today, I will write it down here. Who can I ask for help with this feeling?

YES, I CAN. AND I WILL. WATCH ME.

YES,
#WatchMe
I CAN

DATE: _____

Something I love about myself TODAY:

[ ]

Something I am grateful for TODAY: (Focus on people, relationships, places, experiences - not "things.")

[ ]

I will practice kindness to someone else TODAY by doing/saying/acting:

[ ]

To make my body strong TODAY, I will:

[ ]

Re-write the following affirmations in the space under each phrase:

I AM KIND AND CAPABLE   MY BODY IS STRONG

I AM BRAVE   I LOVE WHO I AM

I AM A BEAUTIFUL PERSON   I AM LOVED BY MANY

How was my day today? (*Great? Good? Hard? Why?*) If I felt a difficult feeling today, I will write it down here. Who can I ask for help with this feeling?

[ ]

YES, I CAN. AND I WILL. WATCH ME.

YES,
#WatchMe
I CAN

DATE: _____

Weekly Reflection + Mindfulness:

My favourite part of the past week was:

> [blank box]

The hardest part of the past week was:

> [blank box]

Mindfulness Challenge:

Lie down on the floor with your hands folded over your belly.
Practice breathing in and out through your nose. Pay attention to how your breath comes in through your nose, travels down your throat, lifts your chest and then allows your belly to rise. This is called the Three-Part Breath.

Focus on the path your breath travels through your nose, filling your lungs and then forcing your belly to rise and lower like a balloon filling and emptying.

Notice your hands rising and falling as you breathe.

Stay focused on the breath path and repeat for ten-15 breaths.

YES, I CAN
#WatchMe

DATE: _____

Something I love about myself TODAY:

Something I am grateful for TODAY: (Focus on people, relationships, places, experiences - not "things.")

I will practice kindness to someone else TODAY by doing/saying/acting:

To make my body strong TODAY, I will:

Re-write the following affirmations in the space <u>under</u> each phrase:

I AM KIND AND CAPABLE   MY BODY IS STRONG

I AM BRAVE   I LOVE WHO I AM

I AM A BEAUTIFUL PERSON   I AM LOVED BY MANY

How was my day today? (*Great? Good? Hard? Why?*) If I felt a difficult feeling today, I will write it down here. Who can I ask for help with this feeling?

YES, I CAN. AND I WILL. WATCH ME.

YES,
#WatchMe
I CAN

DATE: _____

Something I love about myself TODAY:

Something I am grateful for TODAY: (Focus on people, relationships, places, experiences - not "things.")

I will practice kindness to someone else TODAY by doing/saying/acting:

To make my body strong TODAY, I will:

Re-write the following affirmations in the space <u>under</u> each phrase:

I AM KIND AND CAPABLE   MY BODY IS STRONG

I AM BRAVE   I LOVE WHO I AM

I AM A BEAUTIFUL PERSON   I AM LOVED BY MANY

How was my day today? (*Great? Good? Hard? Why?*) If I felt a difficult feeling today, I will write it down here. Who can I ask for help with this feeling?

YES, I CAN. AND I WILL. WATCH ME.

YES.
YES.
#WatchMe
I CAN

DATE: _____

Something I love about myself TODAY:

Something I am grateful for TODAY: (Focus on people, relationships, places, experiences - not "things.")

I will practice kindness to someone else TODAY by doing/saying/acting:

To make my body strong TODAY, I will:

Re-write the following affirmations in the space <u>under</u> each phrase:

I AM KIND AND CAPABLE   MY BODY IS STRONG

I AM BRAVE   I LOVE WHO I AM

I AM A BEAUTIFUL PERSON   I AM LOVED BY MANY

How was my day today? (*Great? Good? Hard? Why?*) If I felt a difficult feeling today, I will write it down here. Who can I ask for help with this feeling?

YES, I CAN. AND I WILL. WATCH ME.

YES,
I CAN
#WatchMe

DATE: _____

Something I love about myself TODAY:

Something I am grateful for TODAY: (Focus on people, relationships, places, experiences - not "things.")

I will practice kindness to someone else TODAY by doing/saying/acting:

To make my body strong TODAY, I will:

Re-write the following affirmations in the space <u>under</u> each phrase:

I AM KIND AND CAPABLE   MY BODY IS STRONG

I AM BRAVE   I LOVE WHO I AM

I AM A BEAUTIFUL PERSON   I AM LOVED BY MANY

How was my day today? (*Great? Good? Hard? Why?*) If I felt a difficult feeling today, I will write it down here. Who can I ask for help with this feeling?

YES, I CAN. AND I WILL. WATCH ME.

YES. I CAN
#WatchMe

DATE: _____

Something I love about myself TODAY:

Something I am grateful for TODAY: (Focus on people, relationships, places, experiences - not "things.")

I will practice kindness to someone else TODAY by doing/saying/acting:

To make my body strong TODAY, I will:

Re-write the following affirmations in the space <u>under</u> each phrase:

I AM KIND AND CAPABLE   MY BODY IS STRONG

I AM BRAVE   I LOVE WHO I AM

I AM A BEAUTIFUL PERSON   I AM LOVED BY MANY

How was my day today? (*Great? Good? Hard? Why?*) If I felt a difficult feeling today, I will write it down here. Who can I ask for help with this feeling?

YES, I CAN. AND I WILL. WATCH ME.

YES,
#WatchMe
I CAN

DATE: _____

Something I love about myself TODAY:

Something I am grateful for TODAY: (Focus on people, relationships, places, experiences - not "things.")

I will practice kindness to someone else TODAY by doing/saying/acting:

To make my body strong TODAY, I will:

Re-write the following affirmations in the space under each phrase:

I AM KIND AND CAPABLE   MY BODY IS STRONG

I AM BRAVE   I LOVE WHO I AM

I AM A BEAUTIFUL PERSON   I AM LOVED BY MANY

How was my day today? (*Great? Good? Hard? Why?*) If I felt a difficult feeling today, I will write it down here. Who can I ask for help with this feeling?

YES, I CAN. AND I WILL. WATCH ME.

YES, I CAN
#WatchMe

DATE:_____

Something I love about myself TODAY:

Something I am grateful for TODAY: (Focus on people, relationships, places, experiences - not "things.")

I will practice kindness to someone else TODAY by doing/saying/acting:

To make my body strong TODAY, I will:

Re-write the following affirmations in the space <u>under</u> each phrase:

I AM KIND AND CAPABLE   MY BODY IS STRONG

I AM BRAVE   I LOVE WHO I AM

I AM A BEAUTIFUL PERSON   I AM LOVED BY MANY

How was my day today? (*Great? Good? Hard? Why?*) If I felt a difficult feeling today, I will write it down here. Who can I ask for help with this feeling?

YES, I CAN. AND I WILL. WATCH ME.

YES,
#WatchMe
I CAN

DATE: _____

Weekly Reflection + Mindfulness:

My favourite part of the past week was:

> (blank box)

The hardest part of the past week was:

> (blank box)

Mindfulness Challenge:

"Waterfall" music meditation.

Grab your music source and some headphones.
Choose a slow, relaxing song if possible.

Find a spot in your bedroom where you can lie on the floor, with your legs in the air, against a wall. (Your body should make an L shape. If you don't know how to visualize this formation, google "legs up the wall yoga").

Close your eyes and allow yourself to get comfortable in this "waterfall" position. Listen to a song or two, and focus on your breathing while you do so. Try to be still for one to two songs.

YES,
#WatchMe
I CAN

DATE: _____

Something I love about myself TODAY:

> [ ]

Something I am grateful for TODAY: (Focus on people, relationships, places, experiences - not "things.")

> [ ]

I will practice kindness to someone else TODAY by doing/saying/acting:

> [ ]

To make my body strong TODAY, I will:

> [ ]

Re-write the following affirmations in the space under each phrase:

I AM KIND AND CAPABLE   MY BODY IS STRONG

I AM BRAVE   I LOVE WHO I AM

I AM A BEAUTIFUL PERSON   I AM LOVED BY MANY

How was my day today? (*Great? Good? Hard? Why?*) If I felt a difficult feeling today, I will write it down here. Who can I ask for help with this feeling?

> [ ]

YES, I CAN. AND I WILL. WATCH ME.

YES, I CAN
#WatchMe

DATE: _____

Something I love about myself TODAY:

Something I am grateful for TODAY: (Focus on people, relationships, places, experiences - not "things.")

I will practice kindness to someone else TODAY by doing/saying/acting:

To make my body strong TODAY, I will:

Re-write the following affirmations in the space <u>under</u> each phrase:

I AM KIND AND CAPABLE   MY BODY IS STRONG

I AM BRAVE   I LOVE WHO I AM

I AM A BEAUTIFUL PERSON   I AM LOVED BY MANY

How was my day today? (*Great? Good? Hard? Why?*) If I felt a difficult feeling today, I will write it down here. Who can I ask for help with this feeling?

YES, I CAN. AND I WILL. WATCH ME.

YES, I CAN
#WatchMe

DATE: _____

Something I love about myself TODAY:

Something I am grateful for TODAY: (Focus on people, relationships, places, experiences - not "things.")

I will practice kindness to someone else TODAY by doing/saying/acting:

To make my body strong TODAY, I will:

Re-write the following affirmations in the space <u>under</u> each phrase:

I AM KIND AND CAPABLE   MY BODY IS STRONG

I AM BRAVE   I LOVE WHO I AM

I AM A BEAUTIFUL PERSON   I AM LOVED BY MANY

How was my day today? (*Great? Good? Hard? Why?*) If I felt a difficult feeling today, I will write it down here. Who can I ask for help with this feeling?

YES, I CAN. AND I WILL. WATCH ME.

YES, I CAN
#WatchMe

DATE: _____

Something I love about myself TODAY:

Something I am grateful for TODAY: (Focus on people, relationships, places, experiences - not "things.")

I will practice kindness to someone else TODAY by doing/saying/acting:

To make my body strong TODAY, I will:

Re-write the following affirmations in the space <u>under</u> each phrase:

I AM KIND AND CAPABLE   MY BODY IS STRONG

I AM BRAVE   I LOVE WHO I AM

I AM A BEAUTIFUL PERSON   I AM LOVED BY MANY

How was my day today? (*Great? Good? Hard? Why?*) If I felt a difficult feeling today, I will write it down here. Who can I ask for help with this feeling?

YES, I CAN. AND I WILL. WATCH ME.

YES,
#WatchMe
I CAN

DATE: _____

Something I love about myself TODAY:

Something I am grateful for TODAY: (Focus on people, relationships, places, experiences - not "things.")

I will practice kindness to someone else TODAY by doing/saying/acting:

To make my body strong TODAY, I will:

Re-write the following affirmations in the space <u>under</u> each phrase:

I AM KIND AND CAPABLE   MY BODY IS STRONG

I AM BRAVE   I LOVE WHO I AM

I AM A BEAUTIFUL PERSON   I AM LOVED BY MANY

How was my day today? (*Great? Good? Hard? Why?*) If I felt a difficult feeling today, I will write it down here. Who can I ask for help with this feeling?

YES, I CAN. AND I WILL. WATCH ME.

YES.
#WatchMe
I CAN

DATE: _____

Something I love about myself TODAY:

Something I am grateful for TODAY: (Focus on people, relationships, places, experiences - not "things.")

I will practice kindness to someone else TODAY by doing/saying/acting:

To make my body strong TODAY, I will:

Re-write the following affirmations in the space <u>under</u> each phrase:

I AM KIND AND CAPABLE   MY BODY IS STRONG

I AM BRAVE   I LOVE WHO I AM

I AM A BEAUTIFUL PERSON   I AM LOVED BY MANY

How was my day today? (*Great? Good? Hard? Why?*) If I felt a difficult feeling today, I will write it down here. Who can I ask for help with this feeling?

YES, I CAN. AND I WILL. WATCH ME.

YES, #WatchMe I CAN

DATE: _____

Something I love about myself TODAY:

Something I am grateful for TODAY: (Focus on people, relationships, places, experiences - not "things.")

I will practice kindness to someone else TODAY by doing/saying/acting:

To make my body strong TODAY, I will:

Re-write the following affirmations in the space <u>under</u> each phrase:

I AM KIND AND CAPABLE   MY BODY IS STRONG

I AM BRAVE   I LOVE WHO I AM

I AM A BEAUTIFUL PERSON   I AM LOVED BY MANY

How was my day today? (*Great? Good? Hard? Why?*) If I felt a difficult feeling today, I will write it down here. Who can I ask for help with this feeling?

YES, I CAN. AND I WILL. WATCH ME.

DATE: _____

Weekly Reflection + Mindfulness:

My favourite part of the past week was:

The hardest part of the past week was:

Mindfulness Challenge:

Sit in a crossed legged position.
Think about your head and face. Tighten all the muscles in your face and count to five, then release them all as you count to five again.

Now tighten all the muscles in both your arms from your shoulders all the way to your hands. Clench your fists and squeeze everything for five seconds, then release everything and count to five again.

Now, your legs. Five seconds tightening/squeezing, five seconds relaxing.

Now, your entire body. Squeeze/tighten EVERYTHING for five seconds, and then relax your entire body.

YES,
#WatchMe
I CAN

DATE: _____

Something I love about myself TODAY:

Something I am grateful for TODAY: (Focus on people, relationships, places, experiences - not "things")

I will practice kindness to someone else TODAY by doing/saying/acting:

To make my body strong TODAY, I will:

Re-write the following affirmations in the space <u>under</u> each phrase:

I AM KIND AND CAPABLE   MY BODY IS STRONG

I AM BRAVE   I LOVE WHO I AM

I AM A BEAUTIFUL PERSON   I AM LOVED BY MANY

How was my day today? (*Great? Good? Hard? Why?*) If I felt a difficult feeling today, I will write it down here. Who can I ask for help with this feeling?

YES, I CAN. AND I WILL. WATCH ME.

YES, I CAN #WatchMe

DATE: _____

Something I love about myself TODAY:

Something I am grateful for TODAY: (Focus on people, relationships, places, experiences - not "things.")

I will practice kindness to someone else TODAY by doing/saying/acting:

To make my body strong TODAY, I will:

Re-write the following affirmations in the space <u>under</u> each phrase:

I AM KIND AND CAPABLE   MY BODY IS STRONG

I AM BRAVE   I LOVE WHO I AM

I AM A BEAUTIFUL PERSON   I AM LOVED BY MANY

How was my day today? (*Great? Good? Hard? Why?*) If I felt a difficult feeling today, I will write it down here. Who can I ask for help with this feeling?

YES, I CAN. AND I WILL. WATCH ME.

YES,
#WatchMe
I CAN

DATE:_____

Something I love about myself TODAY:

Something I am grateful for TODAY: (Focus on people, relationships, places, experiences - not "things.")

I will practice kindness to someone else TODAY by doing/saying/acting:

To make my body strong TODAY, I will:

Re-write the following affirmations in the space <u>under</u> each phrase:

I AM KIND AND CAPABLE   MY BODY IS STRONG

I AM BRAVE   I LOVE WHO I AM

I AM A BEAUTIFUL PERSON   I AM LOVED BY MANY

How was my day today? (*Great? Good? Hard? Why?*) If I felt a difficult feeling today, I will write it down here. Who can I ask for help with this feeling?

YES, I CAN. AND I WILL. WATCH ME.

YES, I CAN
#WatchMe

DATE: _____

Something I love about myself TODAY:

Something I am grateful for TODAY: (Focus on people, relationships, places, experiences - not "things.")

I will practice kindness to someone else TODAY by doing/saying/acting:

To make my body strong TODAY, I will:

Re-write the following affirmations in the space <u>under</u> each phrase:

I AM KIND AND CAPABLE   MY BODY IS STRONG

I AM BRAVE   I LOVE WHO I AM

I AM A BEAUTIFUL PERSON   I AM LOVED BY MANY

How was my day today? (*Great? Good? Hard? Why?*) If I felt a difficult feeling today, I will write it down here. Who can I ask for help with this feeling?

YES, I CAN. AND I WILL. WATCH ME.

YES.
#WatchMe
I CAN

DATE: _____

Something I love about myself TODAY:

_____

Something I am grateful for TODAY: (Focus on people, relationships, places, experiences - not "things.")

_____

I will practice kindness to someone else TODAY by doing/saying/acting:

_____

To make my body strong TODAY, I will:

_____

Re-write the following affirmations in the space <u>under</u> each phrase:

I AM KIND AND CAPABLE   MY BODY IS STRONG

I AM BRAVE   I LOVE WHO I AM

I AM A BEAUTIFUL PERSON   I AM LOVED BY MANY

How was my day today? (*Great? Good? Hard? Why?*) If I felt a difficult feeling today, I will write it down here. Who can I ask for help with this feeling?

_____

YES, I CAN. AND I WILL. WATCH ME.

YES, I CAN
#WatchMe

DATE: _____

Something I love about myself TODAY:

Something I am grateful for TODAY: (Focus on people, relationships, places, experiences - not "things.")

I will practice kindness to someone else TODAY by doing/saying/acting:

To make my body strong TODAY, I will:

Re-write the following affirmations in the space <u>under</u> each phrase:

I AM KIND AND CAPABLE   MY BODY IS STRONG

I AM BRAVE   I LOVE WHO I AM

I AM A BEAUTIFUL PERSON   I AM LOVED BY MANY

How was my day today? (*Great? Good? Hard? Why?*) If I felt a difficult feeling today, I will write it down here. Who can I ask for help with this feeling?

YES, I CAN. AND I WILL. WATCH ME.

YES, #WatchMe I CAN

DATE: _____

Something I love about myself TODAY:

Something I am grateful for TODAY: (Focus on people, relationships, places, experiences - not "things.")

I will practice kindness to someone else TODAY by doing/saying/acting:

To make my body strong TODAY, I will:

Re-write the following affirmations in the space <u>under</u> each phrase:

I AM KIND AND CAPABLE   MY BODY IS STRONG

I AM BRAVE   I LOVE WHO I AM

I AM A BEAUTIFUL PERSON   I AM LOVED BY MANY

How was my day today? (*Great? Good? Hard? Why?*) If I felt a difficult feeling today, I will write it down here. Who can I ask for help with this feeling?

YES, I CAN. AND I WILL. WATCH ME.

YES. I CAN #WatchMe

DATE: _____

Weekly Reflection + Mindfulness:

My favourite part of the past week was:

The hardest part of the past week was:

Mindfulness Challenge:

Lie down in a quiet space and allow your arms and legs to be relaxed.
Close your eyes and start to become aware of your breathing. Practice breathing
in through your nose, and then out through your mouth like you're blowing air
out of a straw.

Breathe in through your nose as you count to four.
Breathe out through your mouth as you count to six.

Continue this in-for-four, out-for-six breathing for ten cycles.

YES, I CAN
#WatchMe

DATE: _____

Something I love about myself TODAY:

[ ]

Something I am grateful for TODAY: (Focus on people, relationships, places, experiences - not "things.")

[ ]

I will practice kindness to someone else TODAY by doing/saying/acting:

[ ]

To make my body strong TODAY, I will:

[ ]

Re-write the following affirmations in the space under each phrase:

I AM KIND AND CAPABLE   MY BODY IS STRONG

I AM BRAVE   I LOVE WHO I AM

I AM A BEAUTIFUL PERSON   I AM LOVED BY MANY

How was my day today? (*Great? Good? Hard? Why?*) If I felt a difficult feeling today, I will write it down here. Who can I ask for help with this feeling?

[ ]

YES, I CAN. AND I WILL. WATCH ME.

YES, I CAN
#WatchMe

DATE: _____

Something I love about myself TODAY:

Something I am grateful for TODAY: (Focus on people, relationships, places, experiences - not "things.")

I will practice kindness to someone else TODAY by doing/saying/acting:

To make my body strong TODAY, I will:

Re-write the following affirmations in the space <u>under</u> each phrase:

I AM KIND AND CAPABLE   MY BODY IS STRONG

I AM BRAVE   I LOVE WHO I AM

I AM A BEAUTIFUL PERSON   I AM LOVED BY MANY

How was my day today? (*Great? Good? Hard? Why?*) If I felt a difficult feeling today, I will write it down here. Who can I ask for help with this feeling?

YES, I CAN. AND I WILL. WATCH ME.

YES, I CAN
#WatchMe

DATE: _____

Something I love about myself TODAY:

Something I am grateful for TODAY: (Focus on people, relationships, places, experiences - not "things.")

I will practice kindness to someone else TODAY by doing/saying/acting:

To make my body strong TODAY, I will:

Re-write the following affirmations in the space <u>under</u> each phrase:

I AM KIND AND CAPABLE   MY BODY IS STRONG

I AM BRAVE   I LOVE WHO I AM

I AM A BEAUTIFUL PERSON   I AM LOVED BY MANY

How was my day today? (*Great? Good? Hard? Why?*) If I felt a difficult feeling today, I will write it down here. Who can I ask for help with this feeling?

YES, I CAN. AND I WILL. WATCH ME.

YES.
#WatchMe
I CAN

DATE: _____

Something I love about myself TODAY:

Something I am grateful for TODAY: (Focus on people, relationships, places, experiences - not "things.")

I will practice kindness to someone else TODAY by doing/saying/acting:

To make my body strong TODAY, I will:

Re-write the following affirmations in the space <u>under</u> each phrase:

I AM KIND AND CAPABLE   MY BODY IS STRONG

I AM BRAVE   I LOVE WHO I AM

I AM A BEAUTIFUL PERSON   I AM LOVED BY MANY

How was my day today? (*Great? Good? Hard? Why?*) If I felt a difficult feeling today, I will write it down here. Who can I ask for help with this feeling?

YES, I CAN. AND I WILL. WATCH ME.

YES
#WatchMe
I CAN

DATE:_____

Something I love about myself TODAY:

Something I am grateful for TODAY: (Focus on people, relationships, places, experiences - not "things.")

I will practice kindness to someone else TODAY by doing/saying/acting:

To make my body strong TODAY, I will:

Re-write the following affirmations in the space <u>under</u> each phrase:

I AM KIND AND CAPABLE   MY BODY IS STRONG

I AM BRAVE   I LOVE WHO I AM

I AM A BEAUTIFUL PERSON   I AM LOVED BY MANY

How was my day today? (*Great? Good? Hard? Why?*) If I felt a difficult feeling today, I will write it down here. Who can I ask for help with this feeling?

YES, I CAN. AND I WILL. WATCH ME.

YES,
#WatchMe
I CAN

DATE: _____

Something I love about myself TODAY:

Something I am grateful for TODAY: (Focus on people, relationships, places, experiences - not "things.")

I will practice kindness to someone else TODAY by doing/saying/acting:

To make my body strong TODAY, I will:

Re-write the following affirmations in the space <u>under</u> each phrase:

I AM KIND AND CAPABLE   MY BODY IS STRONG

I AM BRAVE   I LOVE WHO I AM

I AM A BEAUTIFUL PERSON   I AM LOVED BY MANY

How was my day today? (*Great? Good? Hard? Why?*) If I felt a difficult feeling today, I will write it down here. Who can I ask for help with this feeling?

YES, I CAN. AND I WILL. WATCH ME.

YES, I CAN #WatchMe

DATE: _____

Something I love about myself TODAY:

```

```

Something I am grateful for TODAY: (Focus on people, relationships, places, experiences - not "things.")

```

```

I will practice kindness to someone else TODAY by doing/saying/acting:

```

```

To make my body strong TODAY, I will:

```

```

Re-write the following affirmations in the space <u>under</u> each phrase:

I AM KIND AND CAPABLE   MY BODY IS STRONG

I AM BRAVE   I LOVE WHO I AM

I AM A BEAUTIFUL PERSON   I AM LOVED BY MANY

How was my day today? (*Great? Good? Hard? Why?*) If I felt a difficult feeling today, I will write it down here. Who can I ask for help with this feeling?

```

```

YES, I CAN. AND I WILL. WATCH ME.

YES,
#WatchMe
I CAN

DATE: _____

Weekly Reflection + Mindfulness:

My favourite part of the past week was:

The hardest part of the past week was:

Mindfulness Challenge:

Sit cross legged in a quiet space. Start noticing your breathing and ensure you're breathing only in and out through your nose.

Put one thumb on the edge of one side of your nose, and the other thumb on the other side of your nose.

Close one of your nostrils with your thumb. Inhale a full breath through the open nostril. Hold for three seconds, and then close that nostril and breathe out through the opposite nostril.

Repeat on the other side. Then repeat the cycle ten times.

YES, I CAN
#WatchMe

DATE: _____

Something I love about myself TODAY:

Something I am grateful for TODAY: (Focus on people, relationships, places, experiences - not "things.")

I will practice kindness to someone else TODAY by doing/saying/acting:

To make my body strong TODAY, I will:

Re-write the following affirmations in the space <u>under</u> each phrase:

I AM KIND AND CAPABLE	MY BODY IS STRONG
I AM BRAVE	I LOVE WHO I AM
I AM A BEAUTIFUL PERSON	I AM LOVED BY MANY

How was my day today? (*Great? Good? Hard? Why?*) If I felt a difficult feeling today, I will write it down here. Who can I ask for help with this feeling?

YES, I CAN. AND I WILL. WATCH ME.

YES, I CAN
#WatchMe

DATE: _____

Something I love about myself TODAY:

Something I am grateful for TODAY: (Focus on people, relationships, places, experiences - not "things.")

I will practice kindness to someone else TODAY by doing/saying/acting:

To make my body strong TODAY, I will:

Re-write the following affirmations in the space under each phrase:

I AM KIND AND CAPABLE   MY BODY IS STRONG

I AM BRAVE   I LOVE WHO I AM

I AM A BEAUTIFUL PERSON   I AM LOVED BY MANY

How was my day today? (*Great? Good? Hard? Why?*) If I felt a difficult feeling today, I will write it down here. Who can I ask for help with this feeling?

YES, I CAN. AND I WILL. WATCH ME.

YES,
#WatchMe
I CAN

DATE: _____

Something I love about myself TODAY:

Something I am grateful for TODAY: (Focus on people, relationships, places, experiences - not "things.")

I will practice kindness to someone else TODAY by doing/saying/acting:

To make my body strong TODAY, I will:

Re-write the following affirmations in the space <u>under</u> each phrase:

I AM KIND AND CAPABLE   MY BODY IS STRONG

I AM BRAVE   I LOVE WHO I AM

I AM A BEAUTIFUL PERSON   I AM LOVED BY MANY

How was my day today? (*Great? Good? Hard? Why?*) If I felt a difficult feeling today, I will write it down here. Who can I ask for help with this feeling?

YES, I CAN. AND I WILL. WATCH ME.

YES.
#WatchMe
I CAN

DATE: _____

Something I love about myself TODAY:

Something I am grateful for TODAY: (Focus on people, relationships, places, experiences - not "things.")

I will practice kindness to someone else TODAY by doing/saying/acting:

To make my body strong TODAY, I will:

Re-write the following affirmations in the space <u>under</u> each phrase:

I AM KIND AND CAPABLE   MY BODY IS STRONG

I AM BRAVE   I LOVE WHO I AM

I AM A BEAUTIFUL PERSON   I AM LOVED BY MANY

How was my day today? (*Great? Good? Hard? Why?*) If I felt a difficult feeling today, I will write it down here. Who can I ask for help with this feeling?

YES, I CAN. AND I WILL. WATCH ME.

YES, I CAN
#WatchMe

DATE: _____

Something I love about myself TODAY:

Something I am grateful for TODAY: (Focus on people, relationships, places, experiences - not "things.")

I will practice kindness to someone else TODAY by doing/saying/acting:

To make my body strong TODAY, I will:

Re-write the following affirmations in the space <u>under</u> each phrase:

I AM KIND AND CAPABLE   MY BODY IS STRONG

I AM BRAVE   I LOVE WHO I AM

I AM A BEAUTIFUL PERSON   I AM LOVED BY MANY

How was my day today? (*Great? Good? Hard? Why?*) If I felt a difficult feeling today, I will write it down here. Who can I ask for help with this feeling?

YES, I CAN. AND I WILL. WATCH ME.

DATE: _____

Something I love about myself TODAY:

Something I am grateful for TODAY: (Focus on people, relationships, places, experiences - not "things.")

I will practice kindness to someone else TODAY by doing/saying/acting:

To make my body strong TODAY, I will:

Re-write the following affirmations in the space <u>under</u> each phrase:

I AM KIND AND CAPABLE   MY BODY IS STRONG

I AM BRAVE   I LOVE WHO I AM

I AM A BEAUTIFUL PERSON   I AM LOVED BY MANY

How was my day today? (*Great? Good? Hard? Why?*) If I felt a difficult feeling today, I will write it down here. Who can I ask for help with this feeling?

YES, I CAN. AND I WILL. WATCH ME.

YES I CAN #UWatchMe

DATE: _____

Something I love about myself TODAY:

Something I am grateful for TODAY: (Focus on people, relationships, places, experiences - not "things.")

I will practice kindness to someone else TODAY by doing/saying/acting:

To make my body strong TODAY, I will:

Re-write the following affirmations in the space <u>under</u> each phrase:

I AM KIND AND CAPABLE   MY BODY IS STRONG

I AM BRAVE   I LOVE WHO I AM

I AM A BEAUTIFUL PERSON   I AM LOVED BY MANY

How was my day today? (*Great? Good? Hard? Why?*) If I felt a difficult feeling today, I will write it down here. Who can I ask for help with this feeling?

YES, I CAN. AND I WILL. WATCH ME.

YES,
#WatchMe
I CAN

DATE: _____

Weekly Reflection + Mindfulness:

My favourite part of the past week was:

┌───┐
│   │
│   │
│   │
│   │
│   │
└───┘

The hardest part of the past week was:

┌───┐
│   │
│   │
│   │
│   │
│   │
└───┘

Mindfulness Challenge:

Get on your hands and knees like a cat or dog would stand.
Practice rounding your spine, making a rainbow or C-shape, and then reversing the C and making a horseshoe or U shape.

Pause for a moment and inhale as you make the U shape, and then exhale as you make the rainbow shape.

Repeat this ten times, moving with your breath.

YES
#WatchMe
I CAN

DATE: _____

Something I love about myself TODAY:

[ ]

Something I am grateful for TODAY: (Focus on people, relationships, places, experiences - not "things.")

[ ]

I will practice kindness to someone else TODAY by doing/saying/acting:

[ ]

To make my body strong TODAY, I will:

[ ]

Re-write the following affirmations in the space <u>under</u> each phrase:

I AM KIND AND CAPABLE   MY BODY IS STRONG

I AM BRAVE   I LOVE WHO I AM

I AM A BEAUTIFUL PERSON   I AM LOVED BY MANY

How was my day today? (*Great? Good? Hard? Why?*) If I felt a difficult feeling today, I will write it down here. Who can I ask for help with this feeling?

[ ]

YES, I CAN. AND I WILL. WATCH ME.

YES,
#WatchMe
I CAN

DATE: _____

Something I love about myself TODAY:

Something I am grateful for TODAY: (Focus on people, relationships, places, experiences - not "things.")

I will practice kindness to someone else TODAY by doing/saying/acting:

To make my body strong TODAY, I will:

Re-write the following affirmations in the space <u>under</u> each phrase:

I AM KIND AND CAPABLE   MY BODY IS STRONG

I AM BRAVE   I LOVE WHO I AM

I AM A BEAUTIFUL PERSON   I AM LOVED BY MANY

How was my day today? (*Great? Good? Hard? Why?*) If I felt a difficult feeling today, I will write it down here. Who can I ask for help with this feeling?

YES, I CAN. AND I WILL. WATCH ME.

YES
#UWatchMe
I CAN

DATE: _____

Something I love about myself TODAY:

Something I am grateful for TODAY: (Focus on people, relationships, places, experiences - not "things.")

I will practice kindness to someone else TODAY by doing/saying/acting:

To make my body strong TODAY, I will:

Re-write the following affirmations in the space under each phrase:

I AM KIND AND CAPABLE   MY BODY IS STRONG

I AM BRAVE   I LOVE WHO I AM

I AM A BEAUTIFUL PERSON   I AM LOVED BY MANY

How was my day today? (Great? Good? Hard? Why?) If I felt a difficult feeling today, I will write it down here. Who can I ask for help with this feeling?

YES, I CAN. AND I WILL. WATCH ME.

DATE: _____

Something I love about myself TODAY:

Something I am grateful for TODAY: (Focus on people, relationships, places, experiences - not "things.")

I will practice kindness to someone else TODAY by doing/saying/acting:

To make my body strong TODAY, I will:

Re-write the following affirmations in the space <u>under</u> each phrase:

I AM KIND AND CAPABLE   MY BODY IS STRONG

I AM BRAVE   I LOVE WHO I AM

I AM A BEAUTIFUL PERSON   I AM LOVED BY MANY

How was my day today? (*Great? Good? Hard? Why?*) If I felt a difficult feeling today, I will write it down here. Who can I ask for help with this feeling?

YES, I CAN. AND I WILL. WATCH ME.

YES, I CAN
#WatchMe

DATE: _____

Something I love about myself TODAY:

Something I am grateful for TODAY: (Focus on people, relationships, places, experiences - not "things.")

I will practice kindness to someone else TODAY by doing/saying/acting:

To make my body strong TODAY, I will:

Re-write the following affirmations in the space <u>under</u> each phrase:

I AM KIND AND CAPABLE   MY BODY IS STRONG

I AM BRAVE   I LOVE WHO I AM

I AM A BEAUTIFUL PERSON   I AM LOVED BY MANY

How was my day today? (*Great? Good? Hard? Why?*) If I felt a difficult feeling today, I will write it down here. Who can I ask for help with this feeling?

YES, I CAN. AND I WILL. WATCH ME.

DATE: _____

Something I love about myself TODAY:

Something I am grateful for TODAY: (Focus on people, relationships, places, experiences - not "things.")

I will practice kindness to someone else TODAY by doing/saying/acting:

To make my body strong TODAY, I will:

Re-write the following affirmations in the space <u>under</u> each phrase:

I AM KIND AND CAPABLE   MY BODY IS STRONG

I AM BRAVE   I LOVE WHO I AM

I AM A BEAUTIFUL PERSON   I AM LOVED BY MANY

How was my day today? (*Great? Good? Hard? Why?*) If I felt a difficult feeling today, I will write it down here. Who can I ask for help with this feeling?

YES, I CAN. AND I WILL. WATCH ME.

YES,
#WatchMe
I CAN

DATE: _____

Something I love about myself TODAY:

Something I am grateful for TODAY: (Focus on people, relationships, places, experiences - not "things.")

I will practice kindness to someone else TODAY by doing/saying/acting:

To make my body strong TODAY, I will:

Re-write the following affirmations in the space <u>under</u> each phrase:

I AM KIND AND CAPABLE   MY BODY IS STRONG

I AM BRAVE   I LOVE WHO I AM

I AM A BEAUTIFUL PERSON   I AM LOVED BY MANY

How was my day today? (*Great? Good? Hard? Why?*) If I felt a difficult feeling today, I will write it down here. Who can I ask for help with this feeling?

YES, I CAN. AND I WILL. WATCH ME.

YES,
#WatchMe
I CAN

DATE: _____

Weekly Reflection + Mindfulness:

My favourite part of the past week was:

The hardest part of the past week was:

Mindfulness Practice:

Lie down on the floor with your hands folded over your belly.
Practice breathing in and out through your nose. Pay attention to how your breath comes in through your nose, travels down your throat, lifts your chest and then allows your belly to rise. This is called the Three-Part Breath.

Focus on the path your breath travels through your nose, filling your lungs and then forcing your belly to rise and lower like a balloon filling and emptying.

Notice your hands rising and falling as you breath.

Stay focused on the breath path and repeat for ten to 15 breaths.

YES, I CAN
#WatchMe

DATE: _____

Something I love about myself TODAY:

[ ]

Something I am grateful for TODAY: (Focus on people, relationships, places, experiences - not "things.")

[ ]

I will practice kindness to someone else TODAY by doing/saying/acting:

[ ]

To make my body strong TODAY, I will:

[ ]

Re-write the following affirmations in the space <u>under</u> each phrase:

I AM KIND AND CAPABLE   MY BODY IS STRONG

I AM BRAVE   I LOVE WHO I AM

I AM A BEAUTIFUL PERSON   I AM LOVED BY MANY

How was my day today? (*Great? Good? Hard? Why?*) If I felt a difficult feeling today, I will write it down here. Who can I ask for help with this feeling?

[ ]

YES, I CAN. AND I WILL. WATCH ME.

YES,
#WatchMe
I CAN

DATE: _____

Something I love about myself TODAY:

_____

Something I am grateful for TODAY: (Focus on people, relationships, places, experiences - not "things.")

_____

I will practice kindness to someone else TODAY by doing/saying/acting:

_____

To make my body strong TODAY, I will:

_____

Re-write the following affirmations in the space under each phrase:

I AM KIND AND CAPABLE   MY BODY IS STRONG

I AM BRAVE   I LOVE WHO I AM

I AM A BEAUTIFUL PERSON   I AM LOVED BY MANY

How was my day today? (*Great? Good? Hard? Why?*) If I felt a difficult feeling today, I will write it down here. Who can I ask for help with this feeling?

_____

YES, I CAN. AND I WILL. WATCH ME.

YES, I CAN
#WatchMe

DATE: _____

Something I love about myself TODAY:

```
[                                                                    ]
```

Something I am grateful for TODAY: (Focus on people, relationships, places, experiences - not "things.")

```
[                                                                    ]
```

I will practice kindness to someone else TODAY by doing/saying/acting:

```
[                                                                    ]
```

To make my body strong TODAY, I will:

```
[                                                                    ]
```

Re-write the following affirmations in the space <u>under</u> each phrase:

I AM KIND AND CAPABLE   MY BODY IS STRONG

I AM BRAVE   I LOVE WHO I AM

I AM A BEAUTIFUL PERSON   I AM LOVED BY MANY

How was my day today? (*Great? Good? Hard? Why?*) If I felt a difficult feeling today, I will write it down here. Who can I ask for help with this feeling?

```
[                                                                    ]
[                                                                    ]
[                                                                    ]
[                                                                    ]
```

YES, I CAN. AND I WILL. WATCH ME.

DATE: _____

Something I love about myself TODAY:

_____

Something I am grateful for TODAY: (Focus on people, relationships, places, experiences - not "things.")

_____

I will practice kindness to someone else TODAY by doing/saying/acting:

_____

To make my body strong TODAY, I will:

_____

Re-write the following affirmations in the space <u>under</u> each phrase:

I AM KIND AND CAPABLE   MY BODY IS STRONG

I AM BRAVE   I LOVE WHO I AM

I AM A BEAUTIFUL PERSON   I AM LOVED BY MANY

How was my day today? (*Great? Good? Hard? Why?*) If I felt a difficult feeling today, I will write it down here. Who can I ask for help with this feeling?

_____

YES, I CAN. AND I WILL. WATCH ME.

YES, I CAN
#WatchMe

DATE: _____

Something I love about myself TODAY:

Something I am grateful for TODAY: (Focus on people, relationships, places, experiences - not "things.")

I will practice kindness to someone else TODAY by doing/saying/acting:

To make my body strong TODAY, I will:

Re-write the following affirmations in the space <u>under</u> each phrase:

I AM KIND AND CAPABLE   MY BODY IS STRONG

I AM BRAVE   I LOVE WHO I AM

I AM A BEAUTIFUL PERSON   I AM LOVED BY MANY

How was my day today? (*Great? Good? Hard? Why?*) If I felt a difficult feeling today, I will write it down here. Who can I ask for help with this feeling?

YES, I CAN. AND I WILL. WATCH ME.

YES.
#WatchMe
I CAN

DATE: _____

Something I love about myself TODAY:

Something I am grateful for TODAY: (Focus on people, relationships, places, experiences - not "things.")

I will practice kindness to someone else TODAY by doing/saying/acting:

To make my body strong TODAY, I will:

Re-write the following affirmations in the space <u>under</u> each phrase:

I AM KIND AND CAPABLE   MY BODY IS STRONG

I AM BRAVE   I LOVE WHO I AM

I AM A BEAUTIFUL PERSON   I AM LOVED BY MANY

How was my day today? (*Great? Good? Hard? Why?*) If I felt a difficult feeling today, I will write it down here. Who can I ask for help with this feeling?

YES, I CAN. AND I WILL. WATCH ME.

YES, I CAN
#WatchMe

DATE: _____

Something I love about myself TODAY:

Something I am grateful for TODAY: (Focus on people, relationships, places, experiences - not "things.")

I will practice kindness to someone else TODAY by doing/saying/acting:

To make my body strong TODAY, I will:

Re-write the following affirmations in the space <u>under</u> each phrase:

I AM KIND AND CAPABLE   MY BODY IS STRONG

I AM BRAVE   I LOVE WHO I AM

I AM A BEAUTIFUL PERSON   I AM LOVED BY MANY

How was my day today? (*Great? Good? Hard? Why?*) If I felt a difficult feeling today, I will write it down here. Who can I ask for help with this feeling?

YES, I CAN. AND I WILL. WATCH ME.

DATE: _____

Weekly Reflection + Mindfulness:

My favourite part of the past week was:

>

The hardest part of the past week was:

>

Mindfulness Practice:

"Waterfall" music meditation.
Grab your music source and some headphones.
Choose a slow, relaxing song if possible.

Find a spot in your bedroom where you can lie on the floor, with your legs in the air, against a wall. (Your body should make an L shape. If you don't know how to visualize this formation, google "legs up the wall yoga").

Close your eyes and allow yourself to get comfortable in this "waterfall" position. Listen to a song or two, and focus on your breathing while you do so. Try do be still for one to two songs.

YES,
#WatchMe
I CAN

DATE: _____

Something I love about myself TODAY:

Something I am grateful for TODAY: (Focus on people, relationships, places, experiences - not "things.")

I will practice kindness to someone else TODAY by doing/saying/acting:

To make my body strong TODAY, I will:

Re-write the following affirmations in the space <u>under</u> each phrase:

I AM KIND AND CAPABLE   MY BODY IS STRONG

I AM BRAVE   I LOVE WHO I AM

I AM A BEAUTIFUL PERSON   I AM LOVED BY MANY

How was my day today? (*Great? Good? Hard? Why?*) If I felt a difficult feeling today, I will write it down here. Who can I ask for help with this feeling?

YES, I CAN. AND I WILL. WATCH ME.

YES,
#WatchMe
I CAN

DATE: _____

Something I love about myself TODAY:

Something I am grateful for TODAY: (Focus on people, relationships, places, experiences - not "things.")

I will practice kindness to someone else TODAY by doing/saying/acting:

To make my body strong TODAY, I will:

Re-write the following affirmations in the space <u>under</u> each phrase:

I AM KIND AND CAPABLE   MY BODY IS STRONG

I AM BRAVE   I LOVE WHO I AM

I AM A BEAUTIFUL PERSON   I AM LOVED BY MANY

How was my day today? (*Great? Good? Hard? Why?*) If I felt a difficult feeling today, I will write it down here. Who can I ask for help with this feeling?

YES, I CAN. AND I WILL. WATCH ME.

YES,
#WatchMe
I CAN

DATE: _____

Something I love about myself TODAY:

Something I am grateful for TODAY: (Focus on people, relationships, places, experiences - not "things.")

I will practice kindness to someone else TODAY by doing/saying/acting:

To make my body strong TODAY, I will:

Re-write the following affirmations in the space <u>under</u> each phrase:

I AM KIND AND CAPABLE   MY BODY IS STRONG

I AM BRAVE   I LOVE WHO I AM

I AM A BEAUTIFUL PERSON   I AM LOVED BY MANY

How was my day today? (*Great? Good? Hard? Why?*) If I felt a difficult feeling today, I will write it down here. Who can I ask for help with this feeling?

YES, I CAN. AND I WILL. WATCH ME.

YES, I CAN #WatchMe

DATE: _____

Something I love about myself TODAY:

Something I am grateful for TODAY: (Focus on people, relationships, places, experiences - not "things.")

I will practice kindness to someone else TODAY by doing/saying/acting:

To make my body strong TODAY, I will:

Re-write the following affirmations in the space <u>under</u> each phrase:

I AM KIND AND CAPABLE   MY BODY IS STRONG

I AM BRAVE   I LOVE WHO I AM

I AM A BEAUTIFUL PERSON   I AM LOVED BY MANY

How was my day today? (*Great? Good? Hard? Why?*) If I felt a difficult feeling today, I will write it down here. Who can I ask for help with this feeling?

YES, I CAN. AND I WILL. WATCH ME.

YES,
#WatchMe
I CAN

DATE: _____

Something I love about myself TODAY:

_____

Something I am grateful for TODAY: (Focus on people, relationships, places, experiences - not "things.")

_____

I will practice kindness to someone else TODAY by doing/saying/acting:

_____

To make my body strong TODAY, I will:

_____

Re-write the following affirmations in the space <u>under</u> each phrase:

I AM KIND AND CAPABLE   MY BODY IS STRONG

I AM BRAVE   I LOVE WHO I AM

I AM A BEAUTIFUL PERSON   I AM LOVED BY MANY

How was my day today? (*Great? Good? Hard? Why?*) If I felt a difficult feeling today, I will write it down here. Who can I ask for help with this feeling?

_____

YES, I CAN. AND I WILL. WATCH ME.

YES,
#WatchMe
I CAN

DATE: _____

Something I love about myself TODAY:

Something I am grateful for TODAY: (Focus on people, relationships, places, experiences - not "things.")

I will practice kindness to someone else TODAY by doing/saying/acting:

To make my body strong TODAY, I will:

Re-write the following affirmations in the space <u>under</u> each phrase:

I AM KIND AND CAPABLE   MY BODY IS STRONG

I AM BRAVE   I LOVE WHO I AM

I AM A BEAUTIFUL PERSON   I AM LOVED BY MANY

How was my day today? (*Great? Good? Hard? Why?*) If I felt a difficult feeling
today, I will write it down here. Who can I ask for help with this feeling?

YES, I CAN. AND I WILL. WATCH ME.

YES, I CAN
#WatchMe

DATE: _____

Something I love about myself TODAY:

Something I am grateful for TODAY: (Focus on people, relationships, places, experiences - not "things.")

I will practice kindness to someone else TODAY by doing/saying/acting:

To make my body strong TODAY, I will:

Re-write the following affirmations in the space <u>under</u> each phrase:

I AM KIND AND CAPABLE   MY BODY IS STRONG

I AM BRAVE   I LOVE WHO I AM

I AM A BEAUTIFUL PERSON   I AM LOVED BY MANY

How was my day today? (*Great? Good? Hard? Why?*) If I felt a difficult feeling today, I will write it down here. Who can I ask for help with this feeling?

YES, I CAN. AND I WILL. WATCH ME.

DATE: _____

Weekly Reflection + Mindfulness:

My favourite part of the past week was:

> [blank box]

The hardest part of the past week was:

> [blank box]

Mindfulness Challenge:

Lie down in a quiet space and allow your arms and legs to be relaxed.
Close your eyes and start to become aware of your breathing. Practice breathing
in through your nose, and then out through your mouth like you're blowing air
out of a straw.

Breathe in through your nose as you count to four.
Breathe out through your mouth as you count to six.

Continue this in-for-four, out-for-six breathing for ten cycles.

YES,
#UWatchMe
I CAN

DATE: _____

Something I love about myself TODAY:

Something I am grateful for TODAY: (Focus on people, relationships, places, experiences - not "things.")

I will practice kindness to someone else TODAY by doing/saying/acting:

To make my body strong TODAY, I will:

Re-write the following affirmations in the space <u>under</u> each phrase:

I AM KIND AND CAPABLE   MY BODY IS STRONG

I AM BRAVE   I LOVE WHO I AM

I AM A BEAUTIFUL PERSON   I AM LOVED BY MANY

How was my day today? (*Great? Good? Hard? Why?*) If I felt a difficult feeling today, I will write it down here. Who can I ask for help with this feeling?

YES, I CAN. AND I WILL. WATCH ME.

YES, I CAN
#WatchMe

DATE: _____

Something I love about myself TODAY:

I am grateful for TODAY: (Focus on people, relationships, places, experiences - not "things.")

I will practice kindness to someone else TODAY by doing/saying/acting:

To make my body strong TODAY, I will:

Re-write the following affirmations in the space <u>under</u> each phrase:

I AM KIND AND CAPABLE   MY BODY IS STRONG

I AM BRAVE   I LOVE WHO I AM

I AM A BEAUTIFUL PERSON   I AM LOVED BY MANY

How was my day today? (*Great? Good? Hard? Why?*) If I felt a difficult feeling today, I will write it down here. Who can I ask for help with this feeling?

YES, I CAN. AND I WILL. WATCH ME.

YES,
#WatchMe
I CAN

DATE: _____

Something I love about myself TODAY:

Something I am grateful for TODAY: (Focus on people, relationships, places, experiences - not "things.")

I will practice kindness to someone else TODAY by doing/saying/acting:

To make my body strong TODAY, I will:

Re-write the following affirmations in the space <u>under</u> each phrase:

I AM KIND AND CAPABLE   MY BODY IS STRONG

I AM BRAVE   I LOVE WHO I AM

I AM A BEAUTIFUL PERSON   I AM LOVED BY MANY

How was my day today? (*Great? Good? Hard? Why?*) If I felt a difficult feeling today, I will write it down here. Who can I ask for help with this feeling?

YES, I CAN. AND I WILL. WATCH ME.

YES, I CAN
#WatchMe

DATE: _____

Something I love about myself TODAY:

Something I am grateful for TODAY: (Focus on people, relationships, places, experiences - not "things.")

I will practice kindness to someone else TODAY by doing/saying/acting:

To make my body strong TODAY, I will:

Re-write the following affirmations in the space <u>under</u> each phrase:

I AM KIND AND CAPABLE   MY BODY IS STRONG

I AM BRAVE   I LOVE WHO I AM

I AM A BEAUTIFUL PERSON   I AM LOVED BY MANY

How was my day today? (*Great? Good? Hard? Why?*) If I felt a difficult feeling today, I will write it down here. Who can I ask for help with this feeling?

YES, I CAN. AND I WILL. WATCH ME.

YES,
#WatchMe
I CAN

DATE: _____

Something I love about myself TODAY:

Something I am grateful for TODAY: (Focus on people, relationships, places, experiences - not "things.")

I will practice kindness to someone else TODAY by doing/saying/acting:

To make my body strong TODAY, I will:

Re-write the following affirmations in the space <u>under</u> each phrase:

I AM KIND AND CAPABLE   MY BODY IS STRONG

I AM BRAVE   I LOVE WHO I AM

I AM A BEAUTIFUL PERSON   I AM LOVED BY MANY

How was my day today? (*Great? Good? Hard? Why?*) If I felt a difficult feeling today, I will write it down here. Who can I ask for help with this feeling?

YES, I CAN. AND I WILL. WATCH ME.

YES.
#WatchMe
I CAN

DATE: _____

Something I love about myself TODAY:

Something I am grateful for TODAY: (Focus on people, relationships, places, experiences - not "things.")

I will practice kindness to someone else TODAY by doing/saying/acting:

To make my body strong TODAY, I will:

Re-write the following affirmations in the space <u>under</u> each phrase:

I AM KIND AND CAPABLE   MY BODY IS STRONG

I AM BRAVE   I LOVE WHO I AM

I AM A BEAUTIFUL PERSON   I AM LOVED BY MANY

How was my day today? (*Great? Good? Hard? Why?*) If I felt a difficult feeling today, I will write it down here. Who can I ask for help with this feeling?

YES, I CAN. AND I WILL. WATCH ME.

YES, #WatchMe I CAN

Something I love about myself TODAY:

Something I am grateful for TODAY: (Focus on people, relationships, places, experiences - not "things.")

I will practice kindness to someone else TODAY by doing/saying/acting:

To make my body strong TODAY, I will:

Re-write the following affirmations in the space under each phrase:

I AM KIND AND CAPABLE   MY BODY IS STRONG

I AM BRAVE   I LOVE WHO I AM

I AM A BEAUTIFUL PERSON   I AM LOVED BY MANY

How was my day today? (*Great? Good? Hard? Why?*) If I felt a difficult feeling today, I will write it down here. Who can I ask for help with this feeling?

YES, I CAN. AND I WILL. WATCH ME.

YES,
I CAN
#WatchMe

DATE: _____

Weekly Reflection + Mindfulness:

My favourite part of the past week was:

The hardest part of the past week was:

Mindfulness Challenge:

Get on your hands and knees like a cat or dog would stand.
Practice rounding your spine, making a rainbow or C-shape, and then reversing the C and making a horseshoe or U shape.

Pause for a moment and inhale as you make the U shape, and then exhale as you make the rainbow shape. Repeat this ten times, moving with your breath.

YES,
#WatchMe
I CAN

DATE: _____

Something I love about myself TODAY:

Something I am grateful for TODAY: (Focus on people, relationships, places, experiences - not "things.")

I will practice kindness to someone else TODAY by doing/saying/acting:

To make my body strong TODAY, I will:

Re-write the following affirmations in the space <u>under</u> each phrase:

I AM KIND AND CAPABLE   MY BODY IS STRONG

I AM BRAVE   I LOVE WHO I AM

I AM A BEAUTIFUL PERSON   I AM LOVED BY MANY

How was my day today? (*Great? Good? Hard? Why?*) If I felt a difficult feeling today, I will write it down here. Who can I ask for help with this feeling?

YES, I CAN. AND I WILL. WATCH ME.

YES, I CAN #WatchMe

DATE: _____

Something I love about myself TODAY:

Something I am grateful for TODAY: (Focus on people, relationships, places, experiences - not "things.")

I will practice kindness to someone else TODAY by doing/saying/acting:

To make my body strong TODAY, I will:

Re-write the following affirmations in the space <u>under</u> each phrase:

I AM KIND AND CAPABLE   MY BODY IS STRONG

I AM BRAVE   I LOVE WHO I AM

I AM A BEAUTIFUL PERSON   I AM LOVED BY MANY

How was my day today? (*Great? Good? Hard? Why?*) If I felt a difficult feeling today, I will write it down here. Who can I ask for help with this feeling?

YES, I CAN. AND I WILL. WATCH ME.

YES
#WatchMe
I CAN

DATE: _____

Something I love about myself TODAY:

Something I am grateful for TODAY: (Focus on people, relationships, places, experiences - not "things.")

I will practice kindness to someone else TODAY by doing/saying/acting:

To make my body strong TODAY, I will:

Re-write the following affirmations in the space <u>under</u> each phrase:

I AM KIND AND CAPABLE   MY BODY IS STRONG

I AM BRAVE   I LOVE WHO I AM

I AM A BEAUTIFUL PERSON   I AM LOVED BY MANY

How was my day today? (*Great? Good? Hard? Why?*) If I felt a difficult feeling today, I will write it down here. Who can I ask for help with this feeling?

YES, I CAN. AND I WILL. WATCH ME.

YES, I CAN
#WatchMe

DATE: _____

Something I love about myself TODAY:

Something I am grateful for TODAY: (Focus on people, relationships, places, experiences - not "things.")

I will practice kindness to someone else TODAY by doing/saying/acting:

To make my body strong TODAY, I will:

Re-write the following affirmations in the space <u>under</u> each phrase:

I AM KIND AND CAPABLE   MY BODY IS STRONG

I AM BRAVE   I LOVE WHO I AM

I AM A BEAUTIFUL PERSON   I AM LOVED BY MANY

How was my day today? (*Great? Good? Hard? Why?*) If I felt a difficult feeling today, I will write it down here. Who can I ask for help with this feeling?

YES, I CAN. AND I WILL. WATCH ME.

YES
#WatchMe
I CAN

DATE: _____

Something I love about myself TODAY:

[ ]

Something I am grateful for TODAY: (Focus on people, relationships, places, experiences - not "things.")

[ ]

I will practice kindness to someone else TODAY by doing/saying/acting:

[ ]

To make my body strong TODAY, I will:

[ ]

Re-write the following affirmations in the space <u>under</u> each phrase:

I AM KIND AND CAPABLE   MY BODY IS STRONG

I AM BRAVE   I LOVE WHO I AM

I AM A BEAUTIFUL PERSON   I AM LOVED BY MANY

How was my day today? (*Great? Good? Hard? Why?*) If I felt a difficult feeling today, I will write it down here. Who can I ask for help with this feeling?

[ ]

YES, I CAN. AND I WILL. WATCH ME.

YES.
#WatchMe
I CAN

DATE: _____

Something I love about myself TODAY:

Something I am grateful for TODAY: (Focus on people, relationships, places, experiences - not "things.")

I will practice kindness to someone else TODAY by doing/saying/acting:

To make my body strong TODAY, I will:

Re-write the following affirmations in the space <u>under</u> each phrase:

I AM KIND AND CAPABLE   MY BODY IS STRONG

I AM BRAVE   I LOVE WHO I AM

I AM A BEAUTIFUL PERSON   I AM LOVED BY MANY

How was my day today? (*Great? Good? Hard? Why?*) If I felt a difficult feeling today, I will write it down here. Who can I ask for help with this feeling?

YES, I CAN. AND I WILL. WATCH ME.

YES,
#WatchMe
I CAN

Something I love about myself TODAY:

Something I am grateful for TODAY: (Focus on people, relationships, places, experiences - not "things.")

I will practice kindness to someone else TODAY by doing/saying/acting:

To make my body strong TODAY, I will:

Re-write the following affirmations in the space under each phrase:

I AM KIND AND CAPABLE   MY BODY IS STRONG

I AM BRAVE   I LOVE WHO I AM

I AM A BEAUTIFUL PERSON   I AM LOVED BY MANY

How was my day today? (Great? Good? Hard? Why?) If I felt a difficult feeling today, I will write it down here. Who can I ask for help with this feeling?

YES, I CAN. AND I WILL. WATCH ME.

YES,
#WatchMe
I CAN

DATE: _____

Weekly Reflection + Mindfulness:

My favourite part of the past week was:

The hardest part of the past week was:

Mindfulness Practice:

Sit cross legged in a quiet space. Start noticing your breathing and ensure you're breathing only in and out through your nose.

Put one thumb on the edge of one side of your nose, and the other thumb on the other side of your nose.

Close one of your nostrils with your thumb. Inhale a full breath through the open nostril. Hold for three seconds, and then close that nostril and breathe out through the opposite nostril.

Repeat on the other side. Then repeat the cycle ten times.

YES,
#WatchMe
I CAN

DATE: _____

Something I love about myself TODAY:

Something I am grateful for TODAY: (Focus on people, relationships, places, experiences - not "things.")

I will practice kindness to someone else TODAY by doing/saying/acting:

To make my body strong TODAY, I will:

Re-write the following affirmations in the space <u>under</u> each phrase:

I AM KIND AND CAPABLE   MY BODY IS STRONG

I AM BRAVE   I LOVE WHO I AM

I AM A BEAUTIFUL PERSON   I AM LOVED BY MANY

How was my day today? (*Great? Good? Hard? Why?*) If I felt a difficult feeling today, I will write it down here. Who can I ask for help with this feeling?

YES, I CAN. AND I WILL. WATCH ME.

YES, I CAN
#WatchMe

DATE: _____

Something I love about myself TODAY:

Something I am grateful for TODAY: (Focus on people, relationships, places, experiences - not "things.")

I will practice kindness to someone else TODAY by doing/saying/acting:

To make my body strong TODAY, I will:

Re-write the following affirmations in the space under each phrase:

I AM KIND AND CAPABLE	MY BODY IS STRONG
I AM BRAVE	I LOVE WHO I AM
I AM A BEAUTIFUL PERSON	I AM LOVED BY MANY

How was my day today? (*Great? Good? Hard? Why?*) If I felt a difficult feeling today, I will write it down here. Who can I ask for help with this feeling?

YES, I CAN. AND I WILL. WATCH ME.

YES, #WatchMe I CAN

DATE: _____

Something I love about myself TODAY:

Something I am grateful for TODAY: (Focus on people, relationships, places, experiences - not "things.")

I will practice kindness to someone else TODAY by doing/saying/acting:

To make my body strong TODAY, I will:

Re-write the following affirmations in the space under each phrase:

I AM KIND AND CAPABLE   MY BODY IS STRONG

I AM BRAVE   I LOVE WHO I AM

I AM A BEAUTIFUL PERSON   I AM LOVED BY MANY

How was my day today? (*Great? Good? Hard? Why?*) If I felt a difficult feeling today, I will write it down here. Who can I ask for help with this feeling?

YES, I CAN. AND I WILL. WATCH ME.

YES,
#WatchMe
I CAN

DATE: _____

Something I love about myself TODAY:

Something I am grateful for TODAY: (Focus on people, relationships, places, experiences - not "things.")

I will practice kindness to someone else TODAY by doing/saying/acting:

To make my body strong TODAY, I will:

Re-write the following affirmations in the space <u>under</u> each phrase:

I AM KIND AND CAPABLE   MY BODY IS STRONG

I AM BRAVE   I LOVE WHO I AM

I AM A BEAUTIFUL PERSON   I AM LOVED BY MANY

How was my day today? (*Great? Good? Hard? Why?*) If I felt a difficult feeling
today, I will write it down here. Who can I ask for help with this feeling?

YES, I CAN. AND I WILL. WATCH ME.

YES, #WatchMe I CAN

DATE: _____

Something I love about myself TODAY:

Something I am grateful for TODAY: (Focus on people, relationships, places, experiences - not "things.")

I will practice kindness to someone else TODAY by doing/saying/acting:

To make my body strong TODAY, I will:

Re-write the following affirmations in the space <u>under</u> each phrase:

I AM KIND AND CAPABLE   MY BODY IS STRONG

I AM BRAVE   I LOVE WHO I AM

I AM A BEAUTIFUL PERSON   I AM LOVED BY MANY

How was my day today? (*Great? Good? Hard? Why?*) If I felt a difficult feeling today, I will write it down here. Who can I ask for help with this feeling?

YES, I CAN. AND I WILL. WATCH ME.

YES, I CAN #WatchMe

DATE: _____

Something I love about myself TODAY:

Something I am grateful for TODAY: (Focus on people, relationships, places, experiences - not "things.")

I will practice kindness to someone else TODAY by doing/saying/acting:

To make my body strong TODAY, I will:

Re-write the following affirmations in the space <u>under</u> each phrase:

I AM KIND AND CAPABLE   MY BODY IS STRONG

I AM BRAVE   I LOVE WHO I AM

I AM A BEAUTIFUL PERSON   I AM LOVED BY MANY

How was my day today? (*Great? Good? Hard? Why?*) If I felt a difficult feeling today, I will write it down here. Who can I ask for help with this feeling?

YES, I CAN. AND I WILL. WATCH ME.

YES,
#WatchMe
I CAN

DATE: _____

Something I love about myself TODAY:

Something I am grateful for TODAY: (Focus on people, relationships, places, experiences - not "things.")

I will practice kindness to someone else TODAY by doing/saying/acting:

To make my body strong TODAY, I will:

Re-write the following affirmations in the space <u>under</u> each phrase:

I AM KIND AND CAPABLE   MY BODY IS STRONG

I AM BRAVE   I LOVE WHO I AM

I AM A BEAUTIFUL PERSON   I AM LOVED BY MANY

How was my day today? (*Great? Good? Hard? Why?*) If I felt a difficult feeling today, I will write it down here. Who can I ask for help with this feeling?

YES, I CAN. AND I WILL. WATCH ME.

YES,
#WatchMe
I CAN

DATE: _____

Weekly Reflection + Mindfulness:

My favourite part of the past week was:

The hardest part of the past week was:

Mindfulness Challenge:

Sit in a crossed legged position.

Think about your head and face. Tighten all the muscles in your face and count to five, then release them all as you count to five again.

Now tighten all the muscles in both your arms from your shoulders all the way to your hands. Clench your fists and squeeze everything for five seconds, then release everything and count to five again.

Now, your legs. Five seconds tightening/squeezing, five seconds relaxing.

Now, your entire body. Squeeze/tighten EVERYTHING for five seconds, and then relax your entire body.

YES,
#WatchMe
I CAN

Notes n' stuff:

_____

_____

_____

_____

_____

_____

_____

_____

_____

_____

_____

_____

_____

_____

_____

_____

_____

"Fall seven times; stand up eight."
-Japanese Proverb

YES,
#WatchMe
I CAN

Notes n' stuff:

_____

_____

_____

_____

_____

_____

_____

_____

_____

_____

_____

_____

_____

_____

_____

_____

_____

_____

"You may be the only person left who believes in
you, but it's enough. It takes just *one star* to pierce
a universe of darkness. Never give up."
-Richelle E. Goodrich

Notes n' stuff:

YES,
#WatchMe
I CAN

"Make the most of yourself by fanning the tiny,
inner sparks of possibility into flames of
achievement."
-Golda Meir

YES,
#WatchMe
I CAN

Notes n' stuff:

_____
_____
_____
_____
_____
_____
_____
_____
_____
_____
_____
_____
_____
_____
_____
_____
_____
_____
_____

"Optimism is the faith that leads to
achievement."
-Helen Keller

Notes n' stuff:

YES,
#WatchMe
I CAN

_____

_____

_____

_____

_____

_____

_____

_____

_____

_____

_____

_____

_____

_____

_____

_____

_____

"Your self-esteem won't come from body parts. You
need to step away from the mirror every once in a
while, and look for another reflection, like the one in
the eyes of the people who love you."
-Stacy London

YES,
I CAN
#WatchMe

Notes n' stuff:

_____
_____
_____
_____
_____
_____
_____
_____
_____
_____
_____
_____
_____
_____
_____
_____
_____
_____

"Kindness makes you the most beautiful person
in the world, no matter what you look like."
-Unknown

Notes n' stuff:

YES,
#WatchMe
I CAN

"You are allowed to be both a masterpiece and a work in progress, simultaneously."
-Sophia Bush

YES,
#WatchMe
I CAN

Notes n' stuff:

_____

_____

_____

_____

_____

_____

_____

_____

_____

_____

_____

_____

_____

_____

_____

_____

_____

_____

_____

"When the whole world is silent, even one voice
becomes powerful."
-Malala Yousafzai

Notes n' stuff:

_____

_____

_____

_____

_____

_____

_____

_____

_____

_____

_____

_____

_____

_____

_____

_____

_____

"Most important, in order to find real happiness,
you must learn to love yourself for the totality of
who you are and not just what you look like."
-Portia de Rossi

Notes n' stuff:

_____

_____

_____

_____

_____

_____

_____

_____

_____

_____

_____

_____

_____

_____

_____

_____

_____

_____

"Another person's beauty is not the absence of
your own."
-Unknown

Notes n' stuff:

_____

_____

_____

_____

_____

_____

_____

_____

_____

_____

_____

_____

_____

_____

_____

_____

_____

"It's a beautiful thing to have lungs that allow you to breathe air and legs that allow you to climb mountains, and it's a shame that sometimes we don't realize that's enough."
-Unknown

Notes n' stuff:

_____
_____
_____
_____
_____
_____
_____
_____
_____
_____
_____
_____
_____
_____
_____
_____
_____
_____

"Knowing what must be done does away with fear."
-Rosa Parks

Notes n' stuff:

YES,
#WatchMe
I CAN

"You were born, as you, for a reason."
-Sophia Bush

Notes n' stuff:

_____

_____

_____

_____

_____

_____

_____

_____

_____

_____

_____

_____

_____

_____

_____

_____

_____

"Wanting to be someone else is a waste of the
person you are."
-Marilyn Monroe

Notes n' stuff:

YES,
#WatchMe
I CAN

"The most difficult thing is the decision to act,
the rest is merely tenacity."
-Amelia Earhart

Notes n' stuff:

"You can waste your [life] drawing lines.
Or you can live your life crossing them."
-Shonda Rhimes

Notes n' stuff:

YES,
#WatchMe
I CAN

_____
_____
_____
_____
_____
_____
_____
_____
_____
_____
_____
_____
_____
_____
_____
_____

"I'd rather regret the things I've done than regret
the things I haven't done."
-Lucille Ball

YES,
#WatchMe
I CAN

Notes n' stuff:

_____

_____

_____

_____

_____

_____

_____

_____

_____

_____

_____

_____

_____

_____

_____

_____

_____

_____

"Think like a queen. A queen is not afraid to fail.
Failure is another stepping stone to greatness."
-Oprah

Notes n' stuff:

YES,
#WatchMe
I CAN

_____

_____

_____

_____

_____

_____

_____

_____

_____

_____

_____

_____

_____

_____

_____

_____

_____

"The difference between successful people and others is how long they spend time feeling sorry for themselves."
-Barbara Corcoran

Notes n' stuff:

_____
_____
_____
_____
_____
_____
_____
_____
_____
_____
_____
_____
_____
_____
_____
_____
_____
_____

"If you don't risk anything, you risk even more."
-Erica Jong

Notes n' stuff:

YES,
#UWatchMe
I CAN

_____

_____

_____

_____

_____

_____

_____

_____

_____

_____

_____

_____

_____

_____

_____

_____

_____

"You may not control all the events that happen
to you, but you can decide not to be reduced by
them."
-Maya Angelou

Notes n' stuff:

_____
_____
_____
_____
_____
_____
_____
_____
_____
_____
_____
_____
_____
_____
_____
_____
_____
_____

"You can never leave footprints that last if you
are always walking on tiptoe."
-Leymah Gbowee

Notes n' stuff:

YES,
#WatchMe
I CAN

"If you don't like the road you're walking, start paving another one."
-Dolly Parton

Notes n' stuff:

_____
_____
_____
_____
_____
_____
_____
_____
_____
_____
_____
_____
_____
_____
_____
_____
_____
_____
_____

"Step out of the history that is holding you back.
Step into the new story you are willing to create."
-Oprah Winfrey

Notes n' stuff:

_____
_____
_____
_____
_____
_____
_____
_____
_____
_____
_____
_____
_____
_____
_____
_____

"What you do makes a difference, and you have to decide what kind of difference you want to make."
-Jane Goodall

Notes n' stuff:

YES,
#WatchMe
I CAN

"You wouldn't worry so much about what others
think of you if you realized how seldom they do."
-Eleanor Roosevelt

YES,
#WatchMe
I CAN

Notes n' stuff:

_____

_____

_____

_____

_____

_____

_____

_____

_____

_____

_____

_____

_____

_____

_____

_____

"I am not afraid of storms for I am learning how
to sail my ship."
-Louise May Alcott

Notes n' stuff:

_____

_____

_____

_____

_____

_____

_____

_____

_____

_____

_____

_____

_____

_____

_____

_____

_____

_____

"In order to be irreplaceable one must always be different."
-Coco Chanel

Notes n' stuff:

YES,
#WatchMe
I CAN

"If you don't ask, the answer is always no."
-Nora Roberts

Notes n' stuff:

_____

_____

_____

_____

_____

_____

_____

_____

_____

_____

_____

_____

_____

_____

_____

_____

_____

_____

"People often say that 'beauty is in the eye of the beholder,' and I say that the most liberating thing about beauty is realizing that you are the beholder."
-Salma Hayek

Notes n' stuff:

_____

_____

_____

_____

_____

_____

_____

_____

_____

_____

_____

_____

_____

_____

_____

_____

"The question isn't who is going to let me; it's
who is going to stop me."
-Ayn Rand

Notes n' stuff:

_____
_____
_____
_____
_____
_____
_____
_____
_____
_____
_____
_____
_____
_____
_____
_____

"The more I like me, the less I want to pretend to
be other people."
-Jamie Lee Curtis

Notes n' stuff:

_____

_____

_____

_____

_____

_____

_____

_____

_____

_____

_____

_____

_____

_____

_____

_____

_____

"The only person you should try to be better than
is who you were yesterday."
-Unknown

Notes n' stuff:

_____

_____

_____

_____

_____

_____

_____

_____

_____

_____

_____

_____

_____

_____

_____

_____

_____

_____

"Beauty begins the moment you decide to be
yourself."
-Coco Chanel

Notes n' stuff:

YES,
#WatchMe
I CAN

_____

_____

_____

_____

_____

_____

_____

_____

_____

_____

_____

_____

_____

_____

_____

_____

"Personality begins where comparison leaves off.
Be unique. Be memorable. Be confident. Be
proud."
-Shannon L. Alder

Notes n' stuff:

_____

_____

_____

_____

_____

_____

_____

_____

_____

_____

_____

_____

_____

_____

_____

_____

"Don't waste your energy trying to change opinions… do your thing, and don't care if they like it."
-Tina Fey

Notes n' stuff:

YES,
I CAN
#WatchMe

_____
_____
_____
_____
_____
_____
_____
_____
_____
_____
_____
_____
_____
_____
_____
_____

"You must do the thing you
think you cannot do."
-Eleanor Roosevelt

Hey! You're done! Now what?
Grab a trusted adult and read through this part together.

Wow, you've made it through over eighty days of journaling and weekly mindfulness challenges! Know that this is an amazing accomplishment! Well done, sweet girl.

The journey does not finish with the completion of this journal. Oh no, your journey has only just started! It is my sincere hope that you have spent the past twelve weeks creating the foundation for regular, daily, consistent practices that you can repeat every day for the rest of your life.

Remembering what you are grateful for, writing or saying out loud the things you love about yourself, acknowledging and spreading kindness, writing and speaking positive affirmations...all these things are important tools in your kit that you can use any time. They are always available and you don't even need anything to practice them.

As long as you are always searching for the positive in yourself and in others, you have the ability to make powerful things happen. *Magic.* That's what I called it at the beginning. You can make magic happen when you're in the right headspace to raise your hand, ask questions, be brave, and chase after the goals that you set for yourself.

So, now is the time to consider if you will want to work through another twelve week journal, or if you think you can manage to continue a practice like this (or at least, some elements of it) on a daily basis without guidance.

Now, the most important part: sit for a minute and feel proud that you've accomplished this project. Second most important: give your parents a squeeze and thank them for taking a chance on this experience for you, and giving you the space to get to know yourself a little better.

You have amazing people who love you, don't ever forget that!

XO
Courtney

References:

1. Suzanne Daley, "Little Girls Lose Their Self-Esteem Way To Adolescence, Study Finds," *The New York Times* (January 1991): nytimes.com/1991/01/09/education/little-girls-lose-their-self-esteem-way-to-adolescence-study-finds.html

2. dove.com/ca/en/dove-self-esteem-project/help-for-parents/talking-about-appearance/how-does-social-media-affect-teens.html

3. Amy Morin, "7 Scientifically Proven Benefits of Gratitude," *Psychology Today* (April 2015): psychologytoday.com/ca/blog/what-mentally-strong-people-dont-do/201504/7-scientifically-proven-benefits-gratitude

4. https://www.randomactsofkindness.org/the-science-of-kindness

5. mindfulnessstudies.com/mindfulness/

About the author

Courtney St Croix is a published author, wellness educator, and mindset transformation coach, and has been a leader in the Canadian fitness industry for the past fourteen years. In 2015, Courtney set out on a personal journey to whole-body self-acceptance, as she recovered from the ultimate female body transformation experience of pre- and post-pregnancy.

Through a long-time struggle with a lack of both confidence and a healthy body image, Courtney wanted to figure out how to create and foster a more confident and self-assured mindset. After becoming a certified Life Purpose and Confidence Coach, she now understands where true confidence is conceived, and aims to share the truths of self-love and self-acceptance with women on a daily basis.

Courtney created the "#MomfidentAF Self-Love Journal" in 2018, and her newest project, "Yes I Can, #WatchMe" is a sequel specific to school-aged girls who are ready to embark on their own self-love journey. This workbook is designed to assist girls with creating a powerful self-esteem and confidence practice, so they are better equipped to feel great about their uniqueness as they transition from elementary to high school.

Courtney lives in Ontario, Canada with her husband Chris, daughter Presley and colossal dog, Molson.

16411748R00084

Made in the USA
Middletown, DE
23 November 2018